D1327488

Discarded

Gilman Co. Public Library

a book about girls, their fears, and their future

girl power in the classroom

by Helen Cordes

⌐ Lerner Publications Company • Minneapolis

Blue Grass Regional Library
Columbia, Tennessee 38401

To Jesse and Zoe, two girls of power who are loved beyond description by their mother and father.

Copyright © 2000 by Lerner Publications Company

All rights reserved. International copyright secured. No part of this book may be reproduced or transmitted in any form or by any means, electronic or mechanical, including photocopying and recording, or by any information storage or retrieval system, without permission in writing from Lerner Publications Company, except for the inclusion of brief quotations in an acknowledged review.

Lerner Publications Company
A Division of Lerner Publishing Group
241 First Avenue North
Minneapolis, MN 55401 U.S.A.

Website address: www.lernerbooks.com

The publisher thanks Sonia Jacobson, who was photographed for the cover of this book.

Library of Congress Cataloging-in-Publication Data

Cordes, Helen, 1954–
    Girl power in the classroom : a book about girls, their fears, and their future / by Helen Cordes.
    Includes bibliographical references.
    Summary: Discusses ways for girls to get the most out of school, including being treated fairly, learning as much as possible, and developing self-esteem.
    ISBN 0–8225–2693–X (alk. paper)
    1. Women—Education (Secondary)—Social aspects—United States—Juvenile literature. 2. Teenage girls—United States—Attitudes—Juvenile literature. 3. Self-esteem—Study and teaching (Secondary)—United States—Juvenile literature. 4. Sex discrimination in education—United States—Juvenile literature. [1. Women—Education. 2. Self-esteem. 3. Sex discrimination in education.] I. Title.
    LC1755.C67   2000
    373.1822—dc21   99–28298

Manufactured in the United States of America
1 2 3 4 5 6 – JR – 05 04 03 02 01 00

Contents

chapter one

Orientation 101

I love school because you learn things and make new friends. There really isn't any subject I don't like—they're all fun!

— *Venice*, 9

How do you feel about school? In writing this book, I asked lots of girls that question. I can think back to what my answer would have been. What would your answer be?

Next question (and this is not a quiz). How do you act in the classroom? Do you speak up when you need to? Ask questions? Act on your own behalf? That's what "girl power" means: a girl feeling free to express herself and choose the options that are best for her.

Lots of girls told me that they don't feel that freedom at school. There are many reasons why.

For starters, peer pressure—the influence of friends and classmates—plays a role. Worrying about what other people think of you is a kind of peer pressure. Making choices based on what your friends think is also peer pressure.

Many girls, like Kristen, 16, don't speak up in class because of peer pressure. "If I ask for help, then people will think I'm stupid," she says. "I'm very quiet in class. I rarely say a word." Other girls don't want to look too smart. If Jenny, 11, answers questions too often, "Everyone will see me as the brain of the class," she says. "I sometimes try to act like I don't know the answer."

Beth, 12, doesn't like to go against the crowd. She says, "I keep quiet because some of the kids in my class laugh at what is said—things I really agree with." Other girls agree that speaking up can get an unwanted reaction. "Girls who talk up in class the way guys do get things on their report cards that say 'Talks too much' and 'Doesn't pay attention in class,'" says Erin, 17.

I'm in [the] talented and gifted [program], but when I got put into the program I was smart and now . . . well, now I'm not.

—Jessica, 13

Are Girls Treated Fairly in School?

Some studies show boys often get more attention from teachers. Sometimes boys dominate class discussion. Students are taught more often about men's achievements than women's achievements. Some people also wonder about the fairness of the tests students take to qualify for college.

Things that Affect How You Feel about School

Lots of things can affect how a girl feels about school—how many friends she thinks she has; how interesting a subject is; how inspiring a coach is.

Here's a twist—what about feeling bad about your looks? Surprisingly—or maybe not—this reason affects lots of girls' feelings about school.

Many girls would prefer to stay inside their lockers on days when they don't look their best. "If I have a 'bad hair day' or just a down day about how I look, then my whole schoolday is shot," Kristen admits. "I try to stay away from social interactions as much as possible."

Kristi, 13, says, "Some days I won't go to school and fake being sick because of how I look in the morning." Jessica, 13, says clothes play a role. "If I wear something no one likes, I'm definitely less likely to call attention to myself by raising my hand in class."

Girls might want to consider allowing themselves to slide a bit when it comes to glitzy fashions and looks. But they should never have to endure the sexual teasing and harassment that can sometimes happen in school. Sexual teasing and harassment refer to unwelcome words or actions, like being called a sexual name or having someone snap your bra. Actions like these keep girls from feeling comfortable and safe at school.

Erin was sexually harassed several times in school. "You start to fear some classes because if a

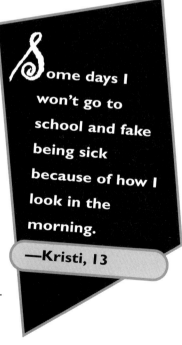

Some days I won't go to school and fake being sick because of how I look in the morning.

—Kristi, 13

certain guy is in it, you never know what they're going to say to you," she explains.

Problems with a girl's family or with other parts of her life "can make things difficult at school," reports Jessica, 16. "It can make paying attention very hard. And it makes your motivation hit the floor."

Why Do More Girls than Boys Lose Self-Esteem?

Some researchers say that a lot of people —people in a girl's school, home, or community—have different expectations for girls than they do for boys. Boys are typically encouraged to pursue goals and be outspoken. Girls, on the other hand, aren't always expected to achieve as much. Sometimes girls are discouraged from being assertive and speaking their minds.

Not the Only One

Any of the above sound familiar? If so, it might feel good to know that you're not alone. As many girls turn twelve and older, they are less and less happy with their school experiences. We asked girls all over the United States and Canada (and other countries, too) how they feel about school and the world around them. Bet you'll find, as you read along, that lots of them are going through the same things you are!

One goal of this book is to look at ways girls can do well in school. By "doing well," we don't mean getting good grades. (Although a few good grades now and then wouldn't hurt!) Mostly, we mean ways that girls can enjoy new things at school, speak their minds, have great friends, feel secure, and gain the confidence they need.

Confidence is going to be a big topic, because it's a big part of school. In one survey of 3,000 kids, about 60 percent of the girls said they were "happy to be me" when they were in elementary school. The same kids took the survey in high school. By then, only about 30 percent of the girls were "happy to be me."

When a person doesn't like herself, she is said to have low self-esteem. And when a person's self-esteem drops, other things in her life drop, too. She might not feel the confidence to try new things. She might not stick up for herself in class or in the hallways. She might think she's not "smart enough."

However, just because some girls lose self-confidence about school doesn't mean every girl does! Besides, a girl can feel differently from one day to the next. Self-esteem isn't a fixed thing. Like your physical health, it changes.

So what's a girl to do to keep up her self-esteem? Look here for ideas! Some of them are fairly simple. We'll learn about the whys and wherefores of common problems. Then we'll learn what girls are doing about them. Of course, no one girl can fix all the stickiest problems. But each time a girl changes her own behavior—even a little!—she automatically gains more ways to tackle the big problems.

Besides, there are a lot of organizations and people who care about girls who are tackling some of those big problems. Girls can consider getting involved as well.

This book includes lots of ideas for getting the most out of your schooldays—including ideas for keeping your self-esteem high. Many come from girls. Others come from adults who care about girls.

I didn't really like high school. In the classroom, boys were often allowed to disrupt class.

—Heather, 19

The ideas focus on:

- how girls can be treated fairly at school;
- how schools can help girls achieve their dreams;
- how girls can feel strong and safe and happy at school.

Getting the most out of school can involve lots more than doing your homework. Feeling good about school means feeling good about the rest of your life, too. To get there, we'll be taking some different kinds of "classes" in this book. Don't worry—there won't be any textbooks or tests involved. We'll look at self-esteem busters and how girls are mowing them down to size. Our goal? Getting girls to have a great time at school— and in life!

chapter two

Self-discovery 202

Everything you do, do it for yourself.
Be a little selfish, because you are the
only one who can sculpt your life into
something great.

—Heather, 18

*I*n this chapter, we're going to talk about self-discovery. Self-discovery means looking inside yourself at the kind of person you truly are, not at the person others may think you should be. Wonder why we'd talk about this in a book about school? Because self-discovery is the key to unlocking the "girl power" in you. We'll hear about how girls judge themselves and about some of the reasons they are judgmental. Then we'll see how girls can let their unique selves be heard—honestly and effectively—in the classroom and beyond.

Who Am I?

Let's begin by doing an inventory. It might be best to get yourself an empty notebook and a pen to do this. In fact, you could consider keeping a diary or journal even after this self-description is done. Many girls say that keeping a diary is a real stress reliever. A diary can be a place to let out thoughts and opinions without anyone else thinking they're dorky or dumb. Diaries are a place to make sure you keep hearing from the *real* you—not the you who might act in different ways to please friends, family, or teachers.

Many girls begin a description of who they are with how they look. A group called the American Association of University Women (AAUW) has done some important studies of girls and education. One study discovered that some girls say that how they look is *the* most important thing about them. The girls in that survey were in grades four through twelve. Some were white girls from middle-income families. These were the girls most likely to believe that looks are the most important thing about themselves.

> *I* keep quiet because some of the kids in my class laugh at what is said.
>
> —Beth, 12

Finding *Your Focus*

When I felt like I was stupid and I thought I was fat when I wasn't, I could never listen to the steps of the evolution of a frog. I was more concerned with whether or not I looked fat in the outfit I was wearing. Standing in front of the class was a nightmare because I thought they would be thinking to themselves, "She could lose some weight."

I'm finally happy with the way I look because I know I'm not fat, and I can concentrate on things that are much more important.

—*Erin*, 17

If a girl's looks are the most important thing, is that a problem? Yes, since most girls are not happy with their looks. Girls especially worry about weight. The Melpomene Institute studies women's health and other women's issues. It talked to girls ages eleven to seventeen about their weight. About 82 percent said they were overweight—even though they were of completely normal sizes.

When girls are not happy with their looks, guess what happens to their self-esteem? It drops. In the AAUW survey, minority girls generally liked their looks more than white girls did. But even they began losing confidence in their looks during middle school and high school.

The size problem has been around for a while for older teens and women. But more younger girls are beginning to believe their bodies are not the "right" size. In still another survey, 40 percent of nine-year-old girls said they were dieting!

Some girls are so unhappy with their body size that they develop eating disorders such as anorexia (starving oneself or not eating enough food to keep healthy) or bulimia (vomiting food). Other girls begin exercising excessively.

The Media Mistake

It's no coincidence that so many girls these days worry about whether they're pretty enough or thin enough. Those feelings may be a result of the images girls see everywhere. The media—TV, magazines, movies, and the like—mostly show beautiful and thin models and actresses. Seeing these women gives girls a very unrealistic version of what a girl's "ideal" looks and body size should be.

Girls can hardly be blamed for finding themselves lacking if they compare themselves to pictures of flawless models. What many girls may not realize is that pictures of models are frequently "fake." A computer can change a photo in any way. It can shave off pounds, shrink a big nose, cover up a pimple, enlarge a chest.

Of course, even before the computer makeover, models have advantages ordinary girls don't have. They get to have each imperfection erased by professional makeup artists who know every trick of the trade. Fair game for comparison? Not!

I have big feet and freckles, and I can't change those things, so why worry about it?

—Rachel, 18

So, as you start describing your looks, try describing them using another standard for comparison. Look at the ordinary girls and women around you. You'll notice some truths about bodies, particularly bodies that are changing into women's bodies. For example, practically all girls will grow thighs and hips bigger than a superscrawny model has. As you know from biology class, wider hips are part of a normal woman's anatomy.

And breasts come in every conceivable shape and size. Check it out by glancing around a swimming pool. Girls who start using ordinary women for comparison often feel better about their looks.

Minority girls are generally happier with their looks because they usually compare themselves with the real girls and women around them, according to a University of Arizona study. Evelyn, 14, finds that to be true. She is Mexican American. Evelyn says, "I feel better about my looks when I'm around my family and community." The white girls around her, says Evelyn, "always say they're fat, but I look at them and think they look fine."

> *I feel better about my looks when I'm around my family and community.*
>
> —Evelyn, 14

What Do I Like about Me?

This is the next question for your inventory. Oddly enough, it's a hard one to answer. Studies show that girls often simply don't believe in their own abilities. When girls become good at something, they often think it's because they're just lucky. They don't take the credit for being competent.

Also, many girls focus more on their failures than they do on their successes. For example, if they got some answers wrong on a test, many girls tend to feel bad about the wrong answers instead of feeling good about all those right answers.

Boys are much more likely than girls to feel "pretty good at a lot of things," according to the AAUW survey. Because boys generally feel more confident about their abilities, they are more likely than girls are to try different things—even when girls and boys are at similar skill levels.

An AAUW survey reported that boys are more likely than girls to feel "pretty good about a lot of things."

Why the difference? Some people who study how boys and girls are raised say the difference starts when children are very little. Little boys are complimented and encouraged more about what they can do, while little girls get many more comments about how they look. Has this ever happened to you? Do you usually get compliments about how you look or what you can do?

Also, girls don't always get the message that girls and women are considered equal to men when they look at the lives of females around them. Most women work. But, as a group, women

earn lower wages than men do. In fact, women in the same kinds of jobs as men still earn an overall seventy-one cents for each dollar a man earns.
At home, even when both parents work, mothers often do most of the housework and handle child care.

The media images of females that girls see show an even grimmer picture of women. On TV, male characters outnumber female characters three to one. Women are usually portrayed in lower-paying jobs such as clerical work, according to a study by Girls, Incorporated (Girls, Incorporated is an organization that sponsors programs and activities for girls at hundreds of local chapters or related organizations.)

Here's what Mary Pipher, author of a book called *Reviving Ophelia,* has to say on this subject. "Girls grow up hearing that girls can be anything," says Pipher. "But then they see in their schools and the rest of the world that girls and women are not valued as much as men in this culture."

Yet feeling proud of themselves is critical for girls. University of Arizona researchers asked girls to describe the "ideal" girl. Many white girls described someone with looks similar to a Barbie doll.

Most African-American girls described an ideal girl as someone with characteristics like "has a good head on her shoulders" and "gets along well with others." It's not surprising that African-American girls have higher self-esteem than white girls do.

"Has a good head" and "gets along well with others." Hmmmm. Aren't those more like things that you look for in a friend and things that others appreciate in you? Most people describe their best friends and favorite classmates in terms that have nothing to do with looks. "My best friend since fifth grade is someone who has always been there for me when I am having problems," says Christina, 13.

Says Liz, 16, "My best friend likes me for who I am, doesn't judge me on my looks, and we get along really well and tell each other everything."

> *My best friend since fifth grade is someone who has always been there for me when I am having problems.*
>
> —Christina, 13

So as you list your abilities and the parts of yourself that you and others like, be sure to include everything you can think of. If you have concluded that you aren't good at a certain thing—think again. Are you sure you're not just focusing on your failings in that area, rather than on your successes? Chances are you have a lot more to be proud of than you thought.

What Don't I Like about Me?

Just because a person focuses on her successes doesn't mean she shouldn't also tackle improvements in needed areas. If you list some part of your body or looks as "needing improvement," fine. But first keep in mind a few things about what can be improved and what can't.

First of all, health experts agree that a person's size has most to do with their genes—the information in their body passed down from their parents. Your eye color and height come from your parents' genes. Well, so does your basic body size. A person's body size is pretty well set at birth. Attempts to make it significantly smaller (or bigger, for the too-skinny) aren't usually effective over time.

Besides, healthy eating and exercise define a good body, not a particular weight. Laura Fraser wrote a book called *Losing It.* She is five feet, six inches tall and weighs 155 pounds. Many might consider her size overweight. But Fraser's doctors certified that Fraser was in great health. She exercises often and eats a low-fat, well-balanced diet. In her book, Fraser includes research on the various diets she and many other women try. She shows that girls who diet rarely keep the weight off permanently.

And remember again about giving yourself realistic goals. Sure, models might look the way you wish you did. But models often have to do unpleasant things such as very strict dieting and hours of daily exercising to keep their bodies thin. Some even have plastic surgery. Many models end up doing some very unhealthy things, such as developing eating disorders or taking dangerous drugs to keep thin.

I **can get depressed after reading fashion magazines, but if I'm with normal people, I feel great.**

—Andrea, 14

As for looks, well, you probably know by now some things can change. (*Yes!* The zits dried up!) Some—like the nose you inherited from Grandpa—don't. Some girls try putting the unchangeable things in perspective.

Other girls remind themselves that others probably pay much less attention than they do to their looks on any given day. "Like last Friday, I had to give a speech in front of the class. I woke up and my hair wouldn't cooperate, and the shirt I wanted to wear wasn't clean," recalls Eva, 13. "I felt like a dork when I stood up, but I got over it when I started talking and realized that I didn't remember what anybody else wore during the last speech they gave, so why would anyone remember what I wore?"

And as for other areas in which you'd like some

self-improvement—maybe better basketball skills or better math grades—go for it! Giving yourself reasonable goals and accomplishing them is a good way to prove yourself to yourself and give the old self-esteem a boost. Just make sure you are creating goals and expectations that are good for *your* needs. As you'll see in our next category, sometimes girls act according to the expectations of others, and that's when trouble can happen.

Do I Feel It's Okay To Be Myself?

Many girls say that particularly as they get into middle school and high school, they feel that they need to change how they usually act. Some, like Melissa, 15, feel they need to act perfect. "I am always expected to be good, never get in trouble, always get good grades," she says. "That's a lot of pressure."

Melissa doesn't usually speak up for herself because "I have this problem with wanting everyone to like me." Katie, 11, feels the same way. "I don't speak up for myself very often because I don't want to hurt anyone's feelings."

Carol Gilligan is a Harvard University psychiatrist who studied middle-school girls. She found that girls who were opinionated and confident in elementary school often changed as they got into middle school. They began speaking and acting in ways they hoped wouldn't offend anyone. For example, girls more likely answered "I don't know" when asked their opinions rather than risk disagreeing with someone or risk not supplying the expected "right" answer.

Forget
the Rules

I don't think the same behavior rules apply to both boys and girls. I would love to just forget about the rules about how I should act and go out and have fun. But I guess, truthfully I have gotten so afraid of getting in trouble by my parents I don't act the way I want. I feel a ton of pressure to keep my grades up, never let them fall. To do good and never wrong. It is pressure and I almost always just wanna go out and rebel.

—*Melissa*, 14

In another study, AAUW researchers looked at ways that girls behave in schools by talking with many different kinds of girls at six middle schools. Researchers found lots of girls like Melissa. These girls usually get good grades and behave in ways considered "traditional" for girls—speaking when called on but rarely offering their opinions and never "making trouble" in class. Girls said they behaved this way to meet the expectations of teachers and parents. As a result, they couldn't always act and speak the way they felt.

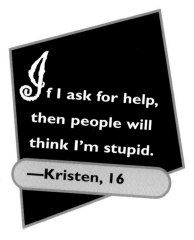

If I ask for help, then people will think I'm stupid.

—Kristen, 16

Another group of girls did speak out loudly and did express opinions. But they often found that others didn't seem to want them to be that way. These girls were often viewed by some teachers and students as "troublemakers." Many of these girls said they felt they had to change those behaviors to be viewed as more acceptable. Some girls even dropped out because of this pressure to change who they are, according to Rutgers University anthropologist Signithia Fordham, who studies African-American girls.

A third group of girls switched the way they behaved according to who they were with, the

AAUW researchers found. This often meant these girls were viewed by others as more successful. But some of these girls ended up wondering who the "real me" was.

As you write down what kind of person you think you are, try to determine whether this person is who you feel you are or who others expect you to be. If you are shy and quiet, that may partly be your personality, but it may also be that you have plenty of things to say but just don't have the nerve to say them all the time. If you like to speak up but feel you're pressured to "pipe down," let your self-description fit who *you* really are.

Nurturing the Real You

It's just nice to know that we're not alone and other girls are going through the same things.

—Meg, 13

Okay, we know who we are— what are we gonna do about it? We'll try acting and talking in ways that nurture the "real" person we are inside. After all, a girl who doesn't feel self-confident enough to be herself loses in two ways. She denies herself important opportunities to learn and to have fun. She also doesn't give other people a chance to get to know things about her and to see what a wonderful, unique person she is!

Let's start by looking at self-confidence, that sometimes hard-to-find quality that more boys seem to have than girls do. It's hard to keep your self-confidence up if you're always reminding yourself of your shortcomings. After all, how many guys do you hear saying things like, "Oh, I look so fat today" or "I'm so dumb—I can't believe I got that test question wrong!" Very many? Probably none.

So, just stop, and encourage your friends to do the same. That's what Emily, 10, did at her school. Whenever a friend would criticize her own efforts, Emily gave her a playful "chop" on the arm to remind her to stop putting herself down. The "Emily chop" has caught on, with other girls using it to keep their friends' confidence up.

Self-confidence also droops when a girl doesn't feel she has the tools to do what she needs and wants to do. Yet lots of girls deny themselves tools—helpful information, useful explanations, and memorable tips—when they won't ask questions in class. Many girls say they wait until after class to ask a friend so "I won't look dumb in class," as Christina, 14, puts it. While this is better than not asking questions at all, it still keeps girls from learning the important skill of getting information at the time it's needed.

Speaking *Up*

Here's how some girls learned to ask questions.
Sarah, 15, decided that the payoff for herself—and
other quiet classmates—was worth speaking up.
"If I don't understand something, then it is better
to feel a little embarrassed for a minute and ask
the question than to feel stupid later," she says.

Being *Yourself*

One of my friends pretends that she isn't as
smart as she is. She used to be at the top
of her class last year, but since we moved to
the high school her marks have really dropped
due to her trying to impress guys by not being
smart. Some other girls I know act really ditzy
when they are around guys, which I just don't
understand. I mean, if I want a guy to like me, I
want them to like me, not some ditzy girl I'm not.

—*Garity*, 14

"Sometimes other people have the same question, and they might even thank you for asking it because they were too afraid to."

Some girls find that talking with other girls about their fears can help them to start talking in class. Melodi, 13, began meeting with other eighth-grade girls at her school's Girls' Club. She discovered other girls were like her and "didn't want to speak up." The girls encourage one another, and Melodi reports that "if I don't understand something now, I just ask."

Marisa, 13, also found that attending weekly meetings of the Girls' Club, which was started by two female teachers, "helped me say more of what I think." Adds Girls' Club member Meg, 13, "It's just nice to know that we're not alone and other girls are going through the same things."

Whether you tackle your talking problem alone or with the help of friends, be sure that you notice any reaction your increased talking in class gets. It's very likely that the thing you may have feared —that other people would think your questions or comments were dumb—just won't happen.

If you do get a bad reaction (say, rolled eyes or a groan from someone who already knows the answer), just remind yourself: that person doesn't know everything either. He or she has to ask questions sometimes, too.

Also, check around to see if others appear to

benefit from your asking the questions. Chances are, other people might be gratefully writing down the teacher's answer or listening to the information you requested.

Do this same kind of reality check when you practice giving your opinions more in class and outside of class. Express your views in a way that is respectful to others. (Hint: *not* "Kim, what you said is so dumb." Try instead: "Kim, I have a different take. Here's what I think.") Bet you'll find that no one thinks less of you or thinks that you're "not nice." And even if someone does think you're too opinionated, well, they're not the kind of person you want in your life anyway. Take it from me—I've spoken out lots of times, and the people who didn't appreciate it weren't friend material anyway.

Some girls who are talkative and opinionated find that their expressiveness can sometimes be used to their advantage. In the AAUW's study, these girls were often good at take-charge positions, such as heading up a class project. For example, Keisha is an eighth-grader whose assertive style of talking led some teachers to say

> *If I don't understand something, then it is better to feel a little embarrassed for a minute and ask the question than to feel stupid later.*
>
> —Sarah, 15

she "had an attitude." Keisha excelled when the principal appointed her to a leadership team of students who helped guide school policy.

Dumping the *Looks Problem*

Getting involved in activities that make you happy and that develop your strengths also has a nice side effect for many girls. "Activities take your mind off looks," says Sarah, 15. "Girls should join them to find people who share the same interests as you, regardless of how you look."

Girls also felt better about their looks when they began looking at beauty "ideals" in new ways. Rachel, 11, watched music videos and TV shows with other girls in her Girls, Incorporated group. As part of the group's "Girls Recast TV" project, the girls talked about the unrealistic looks most women on TV had. This helped Rachel "accept the way I look and understand that I didn't need to look like them."

My best friend likes me for who I am.

—Liz, 16

Other girls find that it helps to simply not look as often at unrealistic views of women. "As soon as I stopped reading magazines like *Seventeen,* I spent a lot less time looking at things I could

never afford and people who I could never be,"
says Rachel, 18. Andrea, 14, discovered that "I can
get depressed after reading fashion magazines,
but if I'm with normal people, I feel great."

Researchers found reactions similar to Andrea's
with other young women. In an Arizona State
University study, young women who often looked
at fashion magazines were dissatisfied with their
bodies and were most likely to have eating
disorders.

As girls resist pressure from themselves and
from our culture to meet unrealistic notions of
beauty, they often find it helps to enlist the aid of
friends. "My true friends make sure I don't get
down on myself about looks," says Brendon, 13.
"And that makes me feel really good."

As you work on letting the real you out, don't
forget to give yourself credit for making changes.
You might even want to chart your progress and
see how you've improved. For example, just for
fun add up the approximate time you spend on a
typical schoolday thinking about your looks.
Include everything, from deciding what you'll
wear to checking mirrors during the day. How'd
you do?

Be sure to do this same exercise in a few
months. Bet you'll have shrunk that time spent on
looks and find you're spending it doing other
things that are a lot more fun.

And try keeping track of other things, too, such as the times you talk in class and give your opinions when you probably wouldn't have in the past. When you log a certain number, give yourself a pat on the back—maybe even have a treat to celebrate!

chapter three

Equality 303

> I do think teachers expect girls to be
> better behaved, but they probably don't
> mean to; it's just that girls are usually
> more well behaved than boys in the first
> place.
>
> —Christina, 14

Step back in time for a minute. Did you know that,
for the first 200 years of American history, most
girls (and nonwhite children, too) were not allowed
to go to school at all? In the late 1700s, girls were
allowed to attend a few schools—but only before
and after school hours for boys. The parents of
those girls had to pay a hefty fee. In the 1800s,
both girls and boys usually went to school, but
they were kept apart. They either went to separate
schools, or they attended all-girls and all-boys
classes in the same building.

In the late 1800s, some people backed coeducation—teaching boys and girls together. Others opposed coeducation. If girls received the same education as boys, they feared, girls would not want to become wives and mothers.

Most elementary schools had become coeducational by the end of the 1800s. But only a few females—mostly wealthy white girls—went on to

How Can Girls Feel Strong and Safe at School?

Some girls report that pressure from friends and classmates can influence decisions about dating and sexual behavior. Many girls complain about mean teasing, from both boys and girls. And more girls are reporting "sexual harassment"— unwanted sexual words or actions—in school hallways. All these things can make it hard for girls to focus on school—or even go to school at all.

high school or college. And even though females and males went to the same schools, they took different classes. Boys took industrial arts and other classes that prepared them for jobs. Girls took homemaking classes that prepared them for being wives and mothers. Also, girls were not allowed to participate in some team sports such as football and baseball.

This went on until about the 1970s. Then Congress passed a law called Title IX (pronounced *Title Nine*). Title IX made it illegal for schools to discriminate against girls and women in school admissions or in classes and activities. Many people believe that Title IX has not been enforced well. Still, the law has given American girls more opportunities in schools. American girls enjoy much better access to education than girls in many other countries do. In fact, fewer than half of the world's girls attend elementary school and high school.

American girls have come a long way. But we need more facts to put together the puzzle of how girls can be happy and successful at school. There are many pieces in that puzzle. In the next few pages, we'll focus on one puzzle piece—what goes on in your classrooms.

I see boys take over classes a lot and dominate the discussion.

—Beth, 12

The main thing we'll check out is whether girls are treated the same as boys at school. Do schools and teachers have the same expectations for both girls and boys? Do they offer equal opportunities to learn?

Here's what some girls—and some researchers—have found. See how their impressions compare with your experiences.

Calling on Boys

"Boys get more attention than girls in my classroom," says Shalane, 9. "They call 'me, me, me, me' out loud and the teacher calls on them," she says.

Beth, 12, finds the same thing in her homeroom. "My teacher calls on the guys with their hands up first, and then calls on the girls," she observes. Boys often end up talking more than girls. "I see boys take over classes a lot and dominate the discussion," says Beth.

Education professors Myra and David Sadker decided to see whether girls and boys got the same deal in America's schools. Along with other people working with them, they watched what went on in hundreds of classrooms, in elementary school through high school. Boys won, they concluded in their book, *Failing at Fairness.* Overall, boys talked more. Teachers called on boys more often—an average of five boys to one girl. Boys also called out answers more.

In some classrooms and situations, boys tend to take over projects, according to both girls and teachers. "When we first got computers in the classroom, the boys tended to take them over and not share information, while the girls would hang back and not get on the computers that much," notes sixth-grade teacher Gayle Beland.

Exploring *Careers*

The National Coalition for Women and Girls in Education took a look at "school-to-work" programs that help students learn about future careers. The study found that many of these programs still encourage girls to explore lower-paying jobs (such as some health-care jobs) while encouraging boys to investigate higher-paying jobs (such as many in industry).

Some girls see boys take over on the school playing fields as well. Anthropology professor Barrie Thorne wrote a book called *Gender Play*. In it, she notes that boys tend to be more competitive in play, while girls tend to play games in which they take turns, such as four-square or kickball.

Researchers also found some reluctance among boys to include girls in teams and games. An Illinois study looked at team games on playgrounds. Most teams—78 percent—were boys only.

In addition, the boys-only games required a lot of space. Barrie Thorne found that boys typically take up about ten times as much playground space as girls do.

The Rewards of Misbehaving

Girls often see boys getting more of the teacher's attention through acting out. "A lot of boys will yell out in class and throw things, and they need to be given more attention than girls because they misbehave more," says Christina, 14.

Beth believes that when girls misbehave, they are more likely

The boys can mouth off, not get busted, but when girls do we get sent to the office.

—Beth, 12

than boys to be scolded or punished. "In most of my classes, the boys can talk and talk and talk, but when girls talk, we get threatened with detention," she says. "The boys can mouth off, not get busted, but when girls do we get sent to the office."

Christina and Beth's observations matched the Sadkers' findings. The Sadkers discovered that boys often got a lot more time from teachers because they misbehaved more. Naturally, boys who misbehaved weren't purposefully taking attention away from others in this way! But the shift in a teacher's attention still had an effect on others. Better-behaved students—many of them girls—got less time and attention. And the Sadkers' studies showed that many teachers expected that girls should behave better than boys.

Giving the Wrong Answer

Many teachers also did a better job of helping boys who got the wrong answer, the Sadkers noted. When boys answered wrong, teachers often let them try again. Sometimes teachers gave clues to the right answer. In contrast, when girls gave the wrong answer, teachers more likely simply told girls they were wrong. Then the teachers would ask someone else.

What about learning new skills? When girls did a new task wrong, teachers often took over, doing the task for them, instead of giving girls more information and having them try again. That's what Jessica, 16, found in her shop class. "My teacher was always taking over whatever I was doing with the saw and told me I was doing it wrong or trying to show me an easier way," she says. "He'd never do that for the guys."

Few Women Role Models

Some girls complain that they have few female role models in the subjects they study at school. "When we looked through our history book, we noticed that the only women mentioned were Pocahontas and Queen Elizabeth I," notes Jessica, 13.

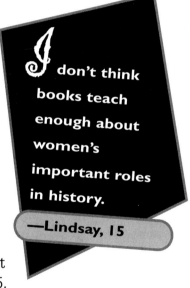

I don't think books teach enough about women's important roles in history.

—Lindsay, 15

"I don't think books teach enough about women's important roles in history," says Lindsay, 15. "That can make girls feel less important."

Studies show that textbooks, while improved in recent years, still focus much more on men. One high school textbook, *A History of the United States,* is more than 1,000 pages long. It focuses on women in fewer than 30 of those pages!

Women's History

Here are some ideas from the National Women's History Project (NWHP) for bringing the rich history of women into your classes.

- For drama or history or English class, you could do a one-girl show that tells the story of a "should-be-famous" woman.
- For art class, make a statue of a woman and explain why she deserves to be honored in that way just as much as the men we see commemorated in statues.
- In journalism class, use an entertaining "Lives of the Oughta-Be Famous" format to interview a partner posing as a noteworthy woman.

The NWHP offers plenty of resources as well as guides that show teachers how to incorporate women's lives into the school curriculum. Your librarian can also point you to women's history books and biographies.

Many girls believe that the lack of women in history results from a past in which "women were not allowed to do things that men could," says Bonnie, 14. But some students of women's history say that plenty of women in the past were leaders, thinkers, and inventors—they just weren't written about. The National Women's History Project (NWHP) has information on hundreds of important women of different cultures throughout history. "Knowing the stories of women's history changes people's lives," says NWHP director Molly Murphy MacGregor, "because it helps them see what is possible."

Whatever the cause, most students know little of accomplished women. When fourth, fifth, and sixth graders were asked to list ten famous men and ten famous women, they listed an average of eleven men and three women. A similar survey of high schoolers showed similar results.

Researchers have also looked at books that are not textbooks—from picture books to teen fiction. Girls are featured as the main character less often than boys. One survey of 1,000 picture books found that boys were shown seven times as often as girls. Girl characters have become stronger in recent years. Still, surveys have shown that girl characters are often still portrayed as less active, less creative, and less independent than boy characters are portrayed.

The reasons for unequal treatment may have to do with lower expectations for girls, say researchers such as the Sadkers. Most women work outside the home both before and after having children. Even so, many people—including some teachers—believe boys will grow up to be their family's "breadwinner." Therefore, boys need more attention at school.

And believe it or not, some people still think boys and men are smarter than girls and women. For example, in one survey, adults were asked to picture an intelligent child. About 71 percent of the men and 57 percent of the women imagined a male child.

It's Hard for Teachers

Many girls found their teachers "give an unequal amount of attention to boys and girls," as Brooke, 15, says. And some girls say that even when teachers want to treat boys and girls equally, teachers often find it hard to involve some girls. "Even if a teacher tries to include the girls in the discussion, the girls might answer a quiet one-word answer," says Jessica, 13. "Girls usually wait until they're spoken to before speaking, unless they're really confident."

Researchers such as the Sadkers have also found that many girls' reluctance to talk has

From studies by Dr. Bernice Sandler, it's been shown that:

- Girls do not participate in classrooms as much as boys do.
- Female teachers make more eye contact with male students than they do with female students.
- Teachers are more likely to nod and gesture in response to comments from male students and to lean forward and assume a position of attentiveness.
- When girls talk, or when the girls considered to be less bright talk, teachers may be inattentive, look at the clock, or shuffle papers.
- Boys are more often called by their given, formal names, such as James or John. Girls are called by the diminutive versions of their names, such as Jody or Suzie.

—*Creative Classroom*

frustrated teachers. Some teachers say that when they try to get girls to talk more, they embarrass the girls. Then the girls are even more reluctant to talk. Some girls also get embarrassed when they give a wrong answer. So a teacher might be hesitant to press a girl to get the right answer.

Girls often were afraid to disagree with teachers. Amanda, 12, says, "I don't speak up when I disagree with teachers because I am afraid I will get in trouble if they don't like how I disagree." The AAUW found that boys were twice as likely as girls to speak up when they disagreed with a teacher.

Often, teachers don't realize that they treat students differently. "I do think teachers expect girls to be better behaved, but they probably don't mean to; it's just that girls are usually more well behaved than boys in the first place," says Christina, 14.

It's not always a student's gender—whether the student is a boy or girl—that might make a teacher treat them differently. University of Michigan psychology professor Jacquelynne Eccles observed classrooms in both junior high and senior high. She found that teachers were giving the most attention to students—both boys and girls—who were getting the best grades.

Barrie Thorne's study of elementary schools led her to another observation: A teacher often favors

What about Girls Only?

Many coed schools have experimented with single-sex classes. Even though both boys and girls attend the school, some classes—particularly classes in math, science, and computer technology—are separated by gender. The idea is to help girls achieve more. Boys may also do better by themselves by becoming less distracted by girls.

These experiments have had mixed results, notes a 1998 report from the AAUW. The best overall solution may be keeping classes coed but making sure that those classrooms are fair to girls. And if classes are kept small, all students are more likely to get the attention they need.

students who are most like himself or herself. Usually, that means students who are middle-class (not from a poor family) and white. In fact, more than 90 percent of America's teachers are white.

The Sadkers emphasize that most teachers try to be fair. Teachers who treat students unequally usually aren't aware of being unfair. The Sadkers point out that many teachers have worked hard to make classrooms more fair to all children. In a large, busy classroom, it's hard for any one teacher to provide equal attention to all students.

What do you find at your school? You're likely to find various situations. Each girl is different, and so is each school. Sometimes girls—not boys—get favored. Kristen, 16, says, "In my school, girls are seen as the ones taking over . . . discussions in class." Dallas, 13, says boys at her school avoid classroom discussions. "Most of the guys don't want to risk being labeled schoolboy," she says. In the end, what matters is that everyone has an equal chance to learn and to feel safe and strong at school.

chapter four

Finding Fairness 404

> Knowing the stories of women's
> history changes people's lives....
> It helps them see what is possible.
> — Molly MacGregor

What's a girl to do if she sees unfair treatment at school? The first thing to do is to get the facts. If you think boys are called on more than girls in a certain class, keep a tally. Note who talks longer, who gets scolded, who gets punished for what. You could even do this as a research paper. Your observations will help show what's really going on. Consider getting others involved. With the help of a teacher, parents, or perhaps the local Parent-Teacher Association (PTA), students can help research fairness. Girls could make it a group project with friends.

Talk to Your Teacher

If students aren't treated equally, talk to your teacher about it. Most teachers welcome input. A teacher might use your information to have a class discussion about fairness. Linda Kekelis, a school consultant, has seen that happen many times. Girls can help keep teachers aware of when boys take over group projects.

Some girls who have found unequal treatment in sports were successful in asking teachers for changes. "The gym teachers were a bit sexist," reports Kellie, 12. "We had to take dance, and the boys took wrestling, but we complained and they made the boys take dance for a week."

Find the Resources

There are plenty of resources that can help teachers achieve gender equality in schools. Linda Kekelis has a company called Academy Street. It is just one of many organizations that help schools start "gender equity" programs. These efforts make sure girls and boys are treated equally.

The Equity Resource Center is funded by the U.S. government. It offers books and other resources for teachers and parents interested in making classrooms fair and fun for all students. Try suggesting to your teacher or principal that they check out these resources.

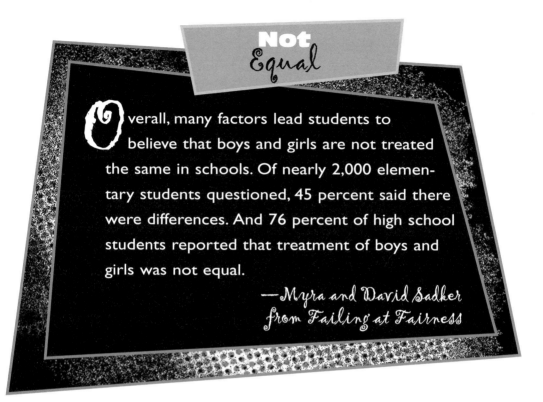

Not
Equal

Overall, many factors lead students to believe that boys and girls are not treated the same in schools. Of nearly 2,000 elementary students questioned, 45 percent said there were differences. And 76 percent of high school students reported that treatment of boys and girls was not equal.

—Myra and David Sadker
from Failing at Fairness

Another resource is the AAUW. This organization also helps teachers and parents. For example, it offers "What's Working for Girls in Schools." This publication outlines classroom programs across the country that are helping girls. It also has many tips for students, parents, and teachers. One is that a teacher take turns calling on boys and girls, including students who don't have their hands up.

Many girls are not as quick as boys to raise their hands. Often, they don't want to risk giving the wrong answer. So the AAUW also suggests that teachers give students more time to raise their hands. This is called "wait time." The teacher asks a question, then waits a few seconds longer than usual. That way, more girls will likely volunteer.

Girls may be able to persuade boys to tone down their competitiveness—particularly if all the girls refuse to play until they do and there aren't enough players to make a team! If not, ask your teacher to remind competitive players that sports should be fun for everyone.

Consider the All-Girls Option

More and more schools offer separate classes for boys and girls in subjects that tend to be dominated by boys. These often include math, science, and computer classes. Teacher Gayle Beland started an all-girls computer class. She found "girls cooperated and shared information in teams," Beland says.

> **Girls usually wait until they're spoken to before speaking, unless they're really confident.**
> —Jessica, 13

Study Role Models

Girls can also make a point of choosing women's accomplishments when thinking of ideas for class projects. The NWHP is a good place to start.

Beland's all-girls class worked together to research notable women. Then they wrote profiles of the women and created a computer database. "The girls really enjoyed learning more about women role models," Beland says. "Most girls felt more confident and competent at the end of the class."

Other teachers have made special efforts to present information about women's accomplishments. 'The majority of the assigned books in my history class are about women," says Beth, 12. "My teacher . . . points out all the neat things women did in history."

> *My teacher points out all the neat things women did in history.*
> —Beth, 12

Be Smart

Consider the possibility that it's often not the grown-ups who have unfair expectations for who is smartest or most capable of success. Surprise! It may be you and your classmates who are at fault.

Some girls think it's uncool for anyone to be smart. Jessica, 13, believes that "being smart isn't a good thing at my school because most of the cool

Putting up with
Being Smart

I'm always the first to answer in class, and I always like the challenge of showing guys that I'm not what they think I am. A lot of guys think that they are better than girls in everything. It really bugs me when a guy says anything stereotypical about girls, and I make a point to correct them. I think it's about time that women come forward and show all the sexist guys that we are equals, always have been, and always will be.

—Garity, 14

people aren't smart. I think some people who are really smart act dumb so they won't be made fun of by popular people."

Studying hard can be even riskier when attracting guys is your goal. Many boys make it clear that girls shouldn't be smart—or at least not openly smart. The perception that guys prefer girls who don't act smart has made some girls change their behavior. "I've often noticed that guys pay a lot more attention to girls who are—or at least act—very dumb," says Alex, 15. "I think they're afraid of a girl being smarter than they are."

"I was a 4.0 student for the first semester, and everyone thought I was a dork who just did homework all day," says Jessica, 13. "However, when I pretended I wasn't smart, all of these boys started noticing me."

Some girls didn't change how they acted. "If you're smart, be smart," says Michelle, 14. "If a guy doesn't like you because you're smart, that just shows how *dumb* [he is]."

Rethink *Stereotypes*

Here's what some minority girls say about stereotypes. Sonya, 15, an African-American girl, finds that "people always seem surprised when you're smart." Yet when minority girls do well, they then may get accused of "acting white," sometimes by other minority students. Whitney, 11, who makes all As, says that she's called a "suckup" and that other students "say I act like a white girl."

Some Asian-American girls are angry about the stereotypes they find. "Everyone thinks that Asians are losers, that they only work hard and that they can't stand up for themselves," says Yong, 14. "That's why everyone asks me for my homework and then picks on me because of my accent."

> *M*y advice for girls is to express their thoughts and not care what people think.
>
> —Jessica, 13

Sound unfair? If you agree, make sure that you don't participate in putting unfair expectations on other students. Encourage your friends to do the same. And while it's not easy to resist peer pressure, take the chance and be yourself. It's got to be easier in the end than being a pretender!

chapter five

Class Action 505

I want to graduate with honors so I can be anything I want—a radiologist, a lawyer, or a nurse.

— Tara, 13

What do you want to be when you grow up? Some girls have a specific goal. "I expect to be a speech pathologist," says Ashley, 12. Other girls aren't sure of the specifics, but they do have a general plan. "I hope to be successful, marry, have kids, and be the best I can be at my job," says Stacey, 17. If you have *no* idea what you want to be, that's absolutely fine. What's important at this time of your life is to stay open to lots of possibilities. After all, no one really knows what they'll do after high school or later on. Even people with very specific goals can end up doing something entirely different from what they'd planned. The only way for you to discover what your interests are is to try new things—and give them your best shot.

Count on *the Future*

Staying open to possibilities may be especially important for girls. A girl who is open to a science career in her future, for example, will likely take science classes when she's in school. Women have all kinds of careers, thanks to people who have

Our Country Needs Girls

It's not only that . . . girls need us; it's that we absolutely need them. How can we imagine, in this highly technical world, that our economy won't collapse if we fail to fully develop half our nation's brainpower?

—Jane Daniels, National Science Foundation

worked to open jobs to women that were off-limits in the past. Girls have choices—from astronaut to zookeeper—that are more varied than ever before.

But sometimes when girls think about the future, they don't seriously consider all job options. They may avoid certain classes—maybe ones that are considered by some to be "guy stuff," like advanced math and science. Girls get just as good—sometimes better—grades as boys do in required math classes. Yet far fewer girls go on to take advanced math. That means fewer girls are qualified for jobs related to math—jobs that often pay quite well.

Some girls plan to depend on the support of a husband when they grow up. In a Colorado survey of girls ages thirteen to seventeen, 81 percent said they did not expect to work outside the home when they had children.

Yes, some women do stay at home with their children. Their husbands bring in the income. But no woman can guarantee that things won't change. A husband can get hurt or lose his job. A couple can get divorced. The person you have to rely on all your life is . . . you.

So how can a girl keep her best options open? We'll look at lots of ways—from taking a more active role in current classes, to checking out some new activities, to simply being "well fueled" with healthy habits. These things will open up a wider array of choices for a girl's future. They will also make her life here and now a lot more satisfying!

Getting the Most Out of School

There's no denying that some classes and teachers are, um, . . . shall we say, less inspiring. But you can't always switch classes. Sometimes girls have to work with what they've got. And given that school makes up the biggest chunk of a day, it's worth it to make classes as enjoyable as possible.

Some girls end up disliking a class because they don't understand the subject. It's not surprising when that frustrating situation makes a girl conclude she doesn't care about the class. "I hate math because I don't understand anything," says Jessica, 13. "But it doesn't matter, because I don't really care."

I **think that the only dumb questions are the ones that aren't asked.**

—Julie, 15

Ask Questions

Of course, the best way to keep from getting lost in a class is to make sure you understand things as they come up. Kristi, 13, ran into trouble last year. "I was afraid of all my teachers, so I wouldn't ask for help," she explains. "I usually brought my work home and asked my sister for help on it or tried to do it myself or with friends." Not asking for help in class just means it will take you longer to do your work at home. And an assignment might not turn out too well if you don't really understand it.

Girls who ask for help right when they need it get a boost. They avoid the confusion and extra work of finding answers later. "If I don't understand something in class, I speak up at the time," says Julie, 15. "I think that the only dumb questions are the ones that aren't asked." And remember the girls from the last chapter who helped one another speak up in class? You can work with a friend or two to encourage one another and make it easier for all of you.

Even if you feel hopelessly behind, there are always ways to catch up. Try asking the teacher for a catch-up plan, even if it's a little embarrassing. Most teachers will be glad that you are making the effort. Or ask a school counselor—that person can point you to programs that all schools must provide for students who need extra help in any area. Even if this involves extra work, isn't that better than feeling frustrated and angry for the entire term?

The second thing for girls to consider is whether they are taking advantage of all the opportunities they can. These opportunities can happen both inside and outside of school. Let's look first at the ones in school.

Do *the Math*

Many girls avoid math and science classes. Math is one of the areas on "standardized tests" (such as the SAT, the PSAT, or the ACT). These tests are required for admission into many colleges.

Science Notes

Math and science are my favorite classes because they're important if you want to be anything. I like science because I learn about nature and different kinds of rocks and about the environment. Boys tease me because I like studying about bugs. I really want to be an archaeologist and discover ancient cities and pre-historic animals.

—Venice, 9

Girls typically score lower than boys in math on standardized tests. That's a problem, because the highest scorers get the best shot at admission to colleges and at scholarships. Doing well can make a big difference in a girl's future.

Chances are, you liked math and science when you were in elementary school. Most elementary-aged kids do. That was one of the findings of the AAUW survey we talked about earlier. The AAUW also found, however, that things change as girls get into their high school years. Far fewer girls in high school said they like math and science. Grades in math and science classes were about the same for girls and boys, the survey found. Even so, girls just didn't believe they were good at math and science. While one in four high school boys believed they were good at math, only one in seven girls did.

Why the difference? There's evidence that math and science classrooms are sometimes not as friendly for girls. Some studies found advanced math and science classrooms more competitive. "Good" students often made fun of people who didn't know the answers right away.

> *I* was afraid of all my teachers, so I wouldn't ask for help.
>
> —Kristi, 13

A National Science Foundation project found that some teachers had lower expectations for girls. "If a boy gets the wrong answer, he is told to work through it. With a female, the teacher does it for her," noted study director Dolores Grayson. The National Science Foundation project tries to help math teachers and computer science teachers correct this gender bias in their teaching.

Believe in *Yourself*

A large part of why many girls don't believe they can do well in math and science is because they don't believe in their abilities. Girls who were good at math attributed their good grades to luck or hard work. When they didn't do well, girls blamed themselves. Boys who were good at math credited their competence. Those who didn't do well didn't blame themselves. Instead, they said that math simply wasn't useful to them. (Think you'll ever have to balance a checkbook?)

What's most important about studies such as the AAUW's is the discovery that girls lost their confidence *before* they started doing badly at math. This proves that girls are not *bad* at math—it's just that many girls are not very confident. What is also interesting about the studies is that the girls who did well in math and science generally had the highest self-esteem.

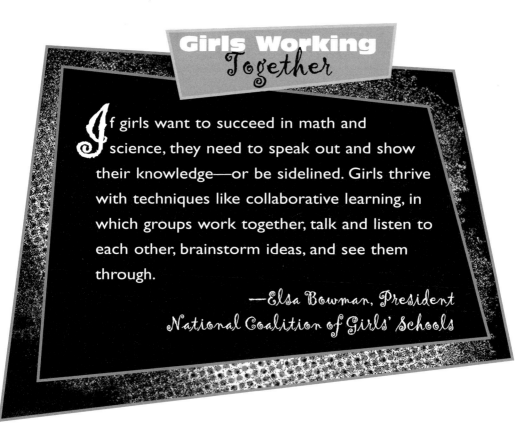

Girls Working Together

*I*f girls want to succeed in math and science, they need to speak out and show their knowledge—or be sidelined. Girls thrive with techniques like collaborative learning, in which groups work together, talk and listen to each other, brainstorm ideas, and see them through.

—Elsa Bowman, President National Coalition of Girls' Schools

Many schools and organizations are trying new ways of teaching subjects like math and science in a more girl-friendly way. Some have tried all-girls classes, which often have higher interest for girls. All-girls classes sometimes result in higher confidence for girls, too.

Organizations such as Girls, Incorporated; Girl Scouts; and the YWCA offer after-school math and science programs. The Girls, Incorporated program is called Operation SMART (which stands for

It All Adds Up

Maybe you don't plan to go to college. Boosting your confidence in math or any other class can still make the class a lot more fun and can have long-term positive effects! Every girl, regardless of her plans, has a right to gain all the skills she can in school.

Science, MAth, and Relevant Technology). In this program, girls do cool experiments and fun math projects and meet women who have careers in math, science, and technology.

Some say confidence is the key to getting high scores on standardized tests. As we learned, research has found that boys and girls taking these tests generally had the same grades in high school. So what happened when these students entered college? The young women typically did just as well or better than the young men! Unfortunately, the young men who got the higher standardized test scores got the scholarships as well.

You can see that standardized test scores don't always relate to a person's success in college. For that reason, some people say the tests are biased against young women and minority students (who also tend to get lower scores).

Criticism from organizations such as FairTest has gotten some positive results. Starting in 1997, the PSAT (which qualifies high school students for National Merit Scholarships) added a writing section. This will likely cause higher scores for girls, because they usually score higher in writing sections. Also, some colleges are relying less on standardized test scores in deciding whom to admit.

When girls simply take the risk to try new things or to speak up for themselves in class, they typically find that nothing bad happens. They just get more competent. These small successes in turn give a girl the self-confidence to try still more things!

Do What You Love

One of the ways girls often find increased self-confidence is through pursuing an interest. It can be sports or music or writing or whatever. "I run and I play viola, and I love doing both of these because it helps me stretch myself to my fullest in all areas," says Lara, 14.

"I used to take dance and kung fu, and I loved doing these," says Kim, 13. "When complimented on a particularly hard move, I felt as if I had conquered Mount Everest. Even today, I draw on that confidence to help me make decisions."

Studies have found that girls who participate in sports generally have higher self-esteem. Girls involved in athletics say they have fun, make friends, learn about working as a team, and discover the payoff of hard work as their skills improve through practice.

Those benefits are the reasons that a Women's Sports Foundation survey found higher grades and graduation rates for young female athletes. It's also interesting to see that confidence in sports is one reason boys say they feel good about themselves.

But any activity a girl likes can raise her self-esteem. "I'm not a big sports person, even though I know they're really great for boosting your confidence," says Alex, 15. "I'm more likely to boost mine by writing a story that kicks—well, you know—and that I'm really proud of."

Girls also find volunteering makes them feel more self-confident. Erin, 17, helps Meals on

> *I'm more likely to boost [my self-esteem] by writing a story that . . . I'm really proud of.*
>
> **—Alex, 15**

Wheels (a program that delivers a hot meal to people who are too old or too sick to cook for themselves). She also volunteers for the human-rights group Amnesty International. "Helping other people always makes me feel a million times better about myself," says Erin.

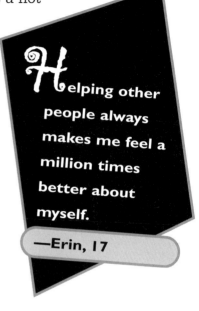

Helping other people always makes me feel a million times better about myself.

—Erin, 17

Amber, 16, agrees. Participating in school activities and volunteering "raises your self-esteem so much," she says. "When you are part of a group, or you are admired by others, it makes you feel very important. You feel as though you can truly make a difference."

Volunteering makes a difference for the people you help, but it also makes a difference for *you*. Thousands of high-school girls volunteer with the Teen Outreach Program (which operates in 25 cities). This program is sponsored by the community group Junior League. Volunteers tutor children, work in parks and hospitals, and do other tasks. Volunteering increased girls' social and academic skills. Volunteers also dropped out of school less often, studies found. And they had 40 percent fewer pregnancies than nonvolunteering teens.

"When teens learn to take care of others, they learn to take care of themselves," says University of Virginia psychologist Joseph Allen, who studied the program.

Listen to Adults *You Respect*

Other girls gain a sense of self-worth when they seek support from others. Studies such as the one conducted by the AAUW find that the approval of adults is one of the most important factors in boosting a young person's self-esteem.

Often girls feel strengthened by a teacher. "My English teacher was a strong woman who made me feel like I could do anything with my mind," says Heather, 18.

Many schools have programs that provide mentors for students. A mentor is usually a person from the local community who meets with a student on a regular basis—typically once a week at school for lunch—to simply listen and talk with the student. Talking with a supportive mentor, especially a woman, can help a girl feel more valued. Big Sisters is another example of a mentoring program. It is available in most communities.

Many girls find support from their families. "My parents want me to do well and tell me they're behind me in whatever I choose to do," says Stephanie, 15.

Families Matter

eeling confident of family love and respect helps a lot. One survey sponsored by the federal government included 90,000 students in grades nine through twelve. It found that teens with family support had better self-esteem than those without that support. The self-confident teens also had fewer problems with depression, drugs, and alcohol.

Mothers may have particular power to inspire daughters. "My mom always tries 110 percent to help me with school- and nonschool-related activities," says Whittnee, 14. "If my grades are bad, she asks me what the problem is and how she can help." When asked, girls most often pick their mothers as the most influential person in their lives.

Get Your ZZZZs

Finally, girls can find some unexpected support for doing their best in school if they remember two things: food and sleep. As students enter the teen years, both boys and girls tend to forget that their bodies need regular pit stops for food and rest.

Girls in particular often ignore their body's need for adequate fuel. That may be because so many girls are concerned about their body size. Many girls say they skip breakfast and lunch to try to lose weight. "I eat a few flakes of cereal in the morning so my mom will think I'm eating, and I bring lunch to school, but I throw it away," says Jessica, 13.

Bonnie, 14, had some bad results when she tried not eating. "In seventh grade, I skipped lunch for about half the year because my best friend did," she recalls. "Then I became friends with another person, and we ate lunch every day. Now I never skip a meal because if I do, I get dizzy and sick."

Bonnie learned what experiments have shown to be true: When people don't get enough food, the deprivation affects both body and mind. Here's what a University of Minnesota study found. A group of men in the study

> Now I never skip a meal because if I do, I get dizzy and sick.
>
> —Bonnie, 14

received only half the food their bodies required. After a few months, they became depressed, angry, and unable to function well in work or social situations.

Sometimes girls don't get adequate food and sleep because they schedule too many activities. Says Melissa, 15, "I practice or have a basketball game every night of the week; then I have homework or choir. I normally never have time for dinner, so I end up eating something like Skittles or having a pop." The result? "I'm always tired at school," says Melissa.

> *I practice or have a basketball game every night of the week.*
>
> —Melissa, 15

Feeling dragged out from too little sleep can affect a girl from the time she wakes up. Laura, 12, puts it this way. "Sometimes I think, 'Oh Laura, you look just beautiful this morning,'" she says. "And then the next day I say, 'I hate the way I look.' It all depends on the amount of sleep I got the night before."

When girls make sure to get enough sleep at least most of the time, they see the difference. Cristina, 13, tries to get a full night's sleep as often as possible. "I feel well conditioned and energized," says Cristina. It just makes sense that everything about school—happiness about looks, friends, and, of course, class performance—is better when the body and brain get rested.

As you can see, there are really a lot of things—from catching enough Zs to trying out lots of opportunities—that can go into improving the schoolday. Give some of these options a try and see for yourself.

chapter six

Self-defense 606

Focus on the aspects of your
personality that make you the person
that you are—whether it be music,
sports, art, writing, whatever.

—*Sarah*, 15

Remember Jessica? I mean the Jessica who said
at the beginning of this book that she used to be
smart, but "Well, now I'm not"? Could a girl really
lose her brainpower? Nope, not possible. But what
is possible is that Jessica stored away her smart-
ness. Why? Because at her school, "most of the
cool people aren't smart."Jessica is not alone in
changing what she says and does for reasons that
have nothing to do with her true self. Peer pressure can be a powerful force. Practically every girl
I heard from in writing this book told of one or
several ways classmates influenced how she acted.

Solving the
Biggest Problem

I think the biggest problem I have had at school was that I really didn't like the way I looked. Between my complexion, my braces, and my glasses, I thought I was really ugly. And I was always getting teased, so my self-esteem was low. But eventually my peers grew up, and my friends stayed with me. Also, having friends from my sports helped.

The advice I have for girls with problems about the way they look is that no matter what other people say about you, feel good about yourself. Find things that are good about you, rather than the ones that are bad. Focus on the aspects of your personality that make you the person that you are—whether it be music, sports, art, writing, whatever. Ignore others and realize that it will get better. Stick with your friends, and the people who like you for who you are.

—Sarah, 15

Many girls felt peer pressure about their looks. "I don't want to go up to the chalkboard if I think that kids are going to laugh at the way I look," says Kate, 14.

Other girls limited their activities because of sexual harassment. "This guy drew pictures of my friend of, well, what he thought she'd look like nude and teased her about being big," says Beth, 12. "He dropped a pencil down the front of her shirt and reached in and took it out. It got so she wouldn't go to classes or any- where he was."

Girls also change how they act because of messages they receive from TV, magazines, movies, and other media. Remember Mary Pipher? In her book, she shows how, more than ever before, girls are sur- rounded by media images of women who are not healthy. Girls see virtually only one version of women—unrealisti- cally thin, beautiful women, usually dressed in revealing, sexy clothes. It's no wonder so many girls try to change how they look and act to match that image.

I like making friends at school, but I don't like being judged by other people because of how I look, act, and dress.

—Megan, 12

But of course few girls will be able to look like supermodels. That sense of failure can make girls less self-confident and not as likely to try new things.

Media images also show women as sex objects—emphasizing only their romantic appeal. Girls are under increasing pressure to look and act sexy, Pipher believes. As a result, girls find themselves acting in ways they are not really comfortable with. Some even end up pregnant.

Girls (as well as boys) are also bombarded with advertising messages. Ads try to convince us that we won't be happy until we buy something, like trendy new clothes or expensive sports shoes. Companies are spending record amounts of money targeting children and teens.

And more than ever before, young people believe the ads. For girls, the message is often that they are only as good as the brands they wear or the things they own. When girls believe the ads, the pressure to look model-perfect just gets worse.

Other stresses can influence how a girl acts, according to Pipher and others. Some of these can be huge problems that require help. A girl may be abusing drugs or alcohol. Or she may feel pressured by classmates to use them. Sexual harassment of girls at school and elsewhere is on the rise. And some girls are sexually abused. Although many of these things happen outside of school, they can have a heavy impact on a girl's happiness at school—or anywhere.

Fighting for Your Best Interests

Whew! With all these messages and pressures, is it any wonder that many girls change how they act in school?

Hold on—don't despair. There is a bunch of good news, too, for girls who are dealing with modern pressures. Lots of people are helping girls come up with solutions for the problems girls face. For example, twenty years ago no one was writing about sexual harassment in schools. People didn't even discuss it. Then many people documented the problem and suggested solutions. These days almost all schools have a policy defining and forbidding sexual harassment.

Also, modern girls know more. They are learning about the pressures they all face. Magazines aimed at girls and young women—from *Girl's Life* to *Glamour*—are featuring more articles about those pressures. Other magazines, such as *New Moon, Blue Jean,* and *Teen Voices,* carry lots of information about important issues for girls. Plus, many books (besides this one, of course) aim to keep girls well informed.

When girls get good information about a problem, they're halfway to having that problem licked. For one thing, being informed is the best way to make the best decision. For another thing, just knowing that other girls face the same problems lets a girl know she's not alone. Then she knows not to blame herself. That's important, according to Jan Maguire, a teacher at an all-girls school. When a girl blames herself, says Maguire, she is more willing to give up.

So, here are some ways girls have learned to create their own self-defense and be the strongest guardians of their best interests.

He dropped a pencil down the front of her shirt and reached in and took it out. It got so she wouldn't go to classes or anywhere he was.

—Beth, 12

Tackling Teasing

Everybody knows that teasing and sexual harassment hurt. Listen to Ashley, 12, who says she is overweight. "I have been called names that kids my age shouldn't even know. It's so painful to have people treat me the way they do." Teasing may happen only as an occasional comment. Even so, words can hurt. Girls report that they are teased about "almost every-

I still feel a deep shame about a teasing incident I participated in many years ago. One girl at my school was often a teasing target because her breasts had developed early. This time, some of my classmates were trying to put a dead bird down her shirt. I laughed and encouraged the others, even though I was troubled by the clearly terrorized look on the girl's face. How I wish I could turn back the clock and redo that moment, this time trying to prevent the cruelty.

—*Helen Cordes*

thing," says Megan, 12. Girls can be teased about being too flat or too busty. They can get teased about getting an A on a school paper or a D. But most often, according to Megan, "When I hear girls being called 'losers,' it's usually for how they dress or weigh."

The teasing makes Megan like school less. "I like making friends at school, but I don't like being judged by other people because of how I look, act, and dress," she says. Most girls would probably agree.

Teasing may be particularly cruel when it's about something a girl has no control over—like the curves that emerge during her teen years. Girls who mature earlier than classmates often get teased. Jenny, 11, notices that. Sometimes she doesn't raise her hand in class because "people might look at me and notice how I've matured."

What would happen if people noticed how Jenny had matured? Teasing about a girl's developing body is sexual harassment. "Some guys would call me up, ones I barely know, and be like, 'You are so hot, you've got some nice jugs,'" says Kristi, 13. Kristi says the comments are "supposed to be a compliment." But the words don't make her feel good. "I just feel more and more ugly," she says.

Girls who lag behind others in body changes may also be teased. Either way, frequent references to a girl's changing body can make her painfully self-conscious. Some girls may get stressed out about a natural process that happens to everyone. Boys, meanwhile, generally welcome their body changes. The changes are proof that they are getting more grown up.

Many girls say they are sexually harassed. In a survey of 4,200 girls in grades two through twelve, nearly 90 percent reported getting sexual comments, gestures, or looks. And 83 percent had been touched, pinched, or grabbed. Most

Keep Telling
If You Need To

My friend and I were sitting at a table at lunch and this boy said to us, "Now which one of you girls is going to suck my penis." We reported it to the teacher, but we noticed she never talked to him. I told my mom, who called the principal. . . . He said he would take care of it.

After a couple of days, I felt he was never talked to, and [my mom] called the principal again and school board members. It turns out there had been other problems with this boy. So . . . starting next year, all teachers from fourth grade through high school will take a seminar on sexual harassment.

harassment happens in school hallways or class-rooms. For almost 40 percent of the girls, the harassment happens repeatedly.

One survey talked to girls in grades eight through eleven about sexual harassment. Over a third of the girls said harassment sometimes made them want to stay away from school. The harassment made them want to be quiet in class and made it harder to concentrate at school.

Some *Solutions*

First, about teasing. Not that it makes it easier to deal with, but girls should keep in mind that most teasers tease because they feel bad about themselves. They put others down to try to make themselves feel better. "I think they're hurting inside over something else—abuse at home or a broken heart—so they come to school and pick on me," writes Kiara, age 12, in *YO!*, a magazine written by teens.

Sometimes people tease even when they know deep down they shouldn't. These teasers just can't resist peer pressure. Annemarie, 14, admits that she's acted this way. "It's not fair that people who are fat or so-called 'losers' are always made fun of," she says. "I do admit to also making fun of them. But everybody does, without thinking about it."

A girl has power over her own actions. So Annemarie's insight leads to a good point: One way to tame teasing is to refuse to participate. You could also—even though it is hard—ask others not to tease. Remind them that teasing hurts them when they are the target. You may have better results if you talk to the teaser when he or she is not around friends. You could even write your comments in a note.

Alex, 15, says that a girl at her school "gets called 'Shamu' [as in the whale] even though she's not even fat." When you are teased, remind yourself of the truth: You are *not* a loser, whale, slut, dork, or whatever else you're being called.

Here's more from someone who has been teased about her appearance. Maybe the teasing is technically correct. This is when you remind yourself that whatever you're being teased about is not the *only* thing about you. Whatever the cruel thing thrown your way, do what Katy, 12, does: "I just turn my head the other way and tell myself all about my good qualities," she says. Friends can really help. Adds Katy, "My

> *I* don't speak up for myself very often because I don't want to hurt anyone's feelings.
>
> —Katie, 11

friends act as cheerleaders to each other and emphasize being beautiful in our own ways."

And make sure that you aren't acting in the *fear* of teasing. For example, Kellie, 12, sometimes dreads going to school. "I am afraid of being ridiculed and stared at by people who think 'Kellie should go on a diet,'" she explains.

Remind yourself that things people tease about happen to them, too. The list of stuff to tease about is so long—a zit outbreak, clothes that aren't the latest fashion, body parts that aren't the "right" size and on and on. Everybody's got *something* on that list.

Good solutions to teasing also come when students talk about the problem together. One project I found out about is called STAGE. In the STAGE project, elementary students help one another learn not to tease. They share stories about teasing and bullying, and then they talk together about how they could handle a similar situation. The kids in STAGE also put on skits showing bully-busting techniques.

Girls can also get together to talk about the common problem of girls teasing other girls. In the Sistahs program in a New York City high school, girls discussed *why* they teased. It turned out that many girls faced challenges in their lives. They were living in poverty, suffering abuse at home, or doing poorly at school. Many girls also felt that they were competing with other girls to see who was the prettiest and could attract the most interest from boys.

When the girls in Sistahs didn't feel successful, they sometimes took out their bad feelings on other girls by teasing them. Just realizing *why* they were teasing made a difference. Girls were then able to give support—not mean words— to one another, says Sistahs founder Mara Benitez.

Maybe your school doesn't have a program such as Sistahs. But girls anywhere can still start to talk to one another honestly about teasing.

> *I don't want to go up to the chalkboard if I think that kids are going to laugh at the way I look.*
>
> **—Katie, 14**

More about
Sexual Harassment

Girls especially need the support of other girls when it comes to sexual teasing. Most schools have rules that forbid unwanted sexual comments, gestures, or touching. When girls know they have the support of friends, they are more likely to take action against harassment. Whether you act on your own or with friends and family, there are three important things to do about sexual harassment:

- Tell the person harassing you to quit.
- If the harassment continues, tell an adult you trust.
- Keep telling until the harassment is stopped.

Try to tell the person to quit the first time harassment happens. If that doesn't stop the behavior, write down details of the harassment. If someone else sees the behavior, ask them to write it down for you as well. Their words will help when you take your problem to a teacher or administrator.

When girls report sexual harassment, it not only ensures that the act is punished, it helps prevent it from happening again. Susan, 14, says that when a popular boy was making frequent sexual comments to girls in many classes, the girls complained to the vice-principal, who suspended the boy. Other students, teachers, and administrators began "keeping a closer eye on him," Susan says.

Getting the help of a parent or counselor early helps a lot. When Katiun, 12, and her mother tackled sexual harassment, their efforts even got a new policy in place to help other students.

Being sexually harassed, teased, or pressured

into sexual activity sends girls a message that others don't respect their bodies. When girls get a lot of these negative messages about their bodies, it's no wonder that they may start believing some of them.

But remember when we discussed how girls should define themselves in ways that were truthful and not based on what others thought? When others give a girl messages that her body doesn't deserve respect, she needs to listen instead to herself. She needs to remind herself that her body is a part of her unique person and is just as important as her mind.

Drugs, Alcohol, and School

When a girl respects and loves her body, she will take good care of it. She'll protect it against things that everybody knows are bad news for bodies, such as drugs and alcohol. That's what Annie wishes she would have done. "I'm only 15, but I'm addicted to drugs. I have been pregnant, and in and out of school since I started," she says.

Getting addicted to drugs has influenced the way Annie feels about her ability to succeed in school. "Something I'm very ashamed to talk about is my brain's abilities," she says. "Since the fourth grade . . . , my IQ tests always came out that I was above average in all my studies by at least two or three school grades. I think if I took one of those tests today I would be average and maybe even slightly below." Although most girls feel some loss of confidence as they enter junior high and high school, girls like Annie perhaps suffer most. "Sometimes I cry when I look at old pictures," she says, "and remember when school life and friends made me happy instead of drugs."

More about the Girl Power Program

This program was started because more girls are using drugs and alcohol. An estimated one in four eighth-grade girls uses alcohol. One in ten of them smokes every day. In Girl Power activities, girls pump up their resistance to drinking and drugs with activities that boost self-esteem. Girls produce cable-access shows, hold Girl Power fashion shows, and give speeches in their communities.

Some girls get help in resisting drug and alcohol abuse with programs such as Friendly PEERsuasion, a Girls, Incorporated program that has girls help other girls. The "Girl Power" program from the federal Health and Human Services Department is another good resource.

Combining School and Sexual Relationships

Girls who respect and love their bodies also make better choices about sexual activity. Particularly as girls get older, they may feel pressured at school to get sexually involved. If you haven't had to make these choices yet, good. You can still think and plan for the future.

"When you start going out with someone, everyone, not just your guy, expects you two to get intimate," says Dallas, 13. This expectation may come because more young people are having sex earlier—over half of students in grades nine through twelve.

Andrea, 16, faced pressure from her boyfriend to become sexually involved. She got pregnant and had a baby. As Andrea found, balancing the needs of a child with the demands of school is an extremely tough act. "Being a sixteen-year-old high school junior with a one-year-old and holding a part-time job is very frustrating and challenging," she says. Andrea's experiences have given her the wisdom of hindsight. "I have learned some positive points from this situation," she says. "I've learned that, if he really loves you, he'll respect [your] decisions and wait on [you] to freely make [your] own choices."

Of course, all human beings have sexual feelings. If they didn't, new babies wouldn't get born! As a girl's hormones increase and she experiences more sexual feelings, she's going to have to do some thinking. She needs to make decisions that are best for her, not decisions based on peer pressure.

Often a girl bases decisions about sexual activity on what is important not only to her but also to her family. A girl may get guidance from her parents or religious advisers. In addition, sometimes a girl finds it useful to talk to a young woman older than herself or to a trusted adult.

That's what Laurie, 15, wishes she had done. Laurie regrets that she became sexually active before she really wanted to. She began having sex at fourteen because "everybody else in my

> $\mathcal{M}$y friends were all so influenced by peer pressure. It was hard to tell what was "right" for me and what was just what everybody else was doing.
>
> —Fontaine, 18

classes said they were, and I didn't want to be left out." Later, she found out that many of her friends had been lying about being sexually active.

Fontaine, 18, also found that she and her friends "were all so influenced by peer pressure. It was hard to tell what was 'right' for me and what was just what everybody else was doing."

Laurie and Fontaine work with a Planned Parenthood program that pairs them with younger girls to discuss the decision-making process. The YWCA has a program called PACT that helps girls make healthy choices about sexual activity. Girls, Incorporated runs a similar program.

Handling *Heavy Problems*

Every girl gets stressed out once in a while. But some girls experience stresses that need serious help. For example, over one million American girls have severe eating problems such as anorexia, bulimia, and compulsive exercising. Fifteen percent of anorexics will die from health problems related to not giving their bodies enough food.

Some girls have serious problems at home, such as parents who abuse drugs and alcohol. Girls are more likely than boys to be sexually abused, meaning that someone, usually someone older, makes her participate in a sexual activity when she doesn't want to. Becoming pregnant or contracting a sexually transmitted disease are other serious problems that affect a girl's health, state of mind, success in school, and dreams for the future. As a result of problems like these, many girls suffer from depression. Some try suicide.

For girls with any of these problems, finding help is critical. A school counselor is a good place to start. She or he can point you to many resources in your community. Otherwise, girls should talk to trusted family members or other trusted adults. A toll-free hotline, 1–800–4–A–CHILD, will direct girls to the help they need.

Talking to someone about bad problems is critical, says Kristen, 16. "Please, please find someone who you can talk to and trust," she says. "I know it sounds corny and hard to do, but it could make a world of difference."

chapter seven

Self-ishness 707

In a few years I will finally be able to
fulfill my dreams.

— *Brandy*, 13

When's the last time someone said you *should* be
selfish? Never? Well, here's to the idea that girls
think of themselves and their best interests every
day—in the classroom and wherever else they are!
Being Self-ish is not the same as being selfish—it's
simply a matter of listening to the needs of your
true Self and making sure that what you do is best
for you. And being Self-ish can happen at the same
time that you continue being a kind person and a
good friend.

It's All about *Your Self*

In the classroom, being Self-ish can mean many things. For one, it means letting your Self feel free to give opinions and to ask whatever questions you might have. That's not always a popular move. But it can help ensure that you learn the most you can.

You Are the One *Who Chooses*

Everything you do, do it for yourself. Be a little selfish, because you are the only one who can sculpt your life into something great. If you are being abused, tell someone. If they don't listen, tell someone else. No matter who you are—cheerleader, bookworm, female athlete, or oddball—you are beautiful! People will say and do whatever they want, but you are the one who chooses how to react.

—*Heather, 18*

"I always make sure my voice is heard," says Brandy, 13. "Some people say I talk too much, but I think kids should speak up more." Being Self-ish has helped Brandy enjoy school and feel confident about her goals. "I love school because without it, I wouldn't be able to go to college and become a doctor," she says. "In a few years I will finally be able to fulfill my dreams."

Being Self-ish in class also means letting yourself be proud—of all your talents and accomplishments, big or small. Boosting your pride can help you when you hit more difficult times (say you're having friendship problems) by reminding you that you have lots of things going *right* for you.

And girls should make sure they give themselves credit for abilities other than those connected with book learning. "I like school because I learn a lot of things and not just in the academic sense," says Minna, 18. "School prepares me for the future because I learn how to make decisions and how to deal with different people and improve my socializing skills."

School prepares me for the future because I learn how to make decisions and how to deal with different people.

—Minna, 18

Minna has what's called EQ—Emotional Intelligence. Such skills serve girls well later in many situations, such as supervising people as a manager.

When choosing optional classes and extracurricular activities, a Self-ish girl chooses the ones most rewarding to her. She doesn't simply go with what her friends are doing. Amber, 16, picked band. She found band was "a group that makes you feel wanted. People are there not because they have to but because they want to."

Of course, a Self-ish girl speaks up and takes advantage of opportunities in nonschool organizations, too. In a Girl Scout survey, girls were asked to compare Girl Scouts with school. They said they could lead projects and make decisions about the group much more often in Girl Scouts than they could at school.

A Self-ish girl doesn't let insecurities about her looks get in the way of enjoying school or anything else. Remember, a girl is much more than the combination of her looks and size. Recognizing and loving her total self brings a big payoff.

Strong friendships can help you through almost anything, whether it be a girl from school, a sister or brother, or even a parent.

—Elizabeth, 16

Katrina, 14, sees that payoff in her friend, Jennie. "Jennie isn't as thin or pretty as she'd like to be, but she loves herself enough to make others love her as well," says Katrina. "She doesn't let her inhibitions about her appearance affect the way she acts and shows her colorful personality."

A Self-ish girl makes time to recharge herself and fight off stress. Many girls find diary writing a huge stress reliever. Kate, 14, uses her diary to make better future decisions as well. "After I finish steaming off by writing down my feelings and reactions, I read what I wrote and see if I should have done stuff differently," she says. Other girls simply put aside time to reflect and relax. "I do some yoga stretches and cleansing of my mind," says Vida, 12. "They make me feel better."

The simplest stress-buster is just giving yourself a break. "I have done some stupid things, and many good, smart things," says Samantha, 17. "I think the good outnumber the bad, and even if it didn't, I know that I am still truly good at heart."

Many girls make sure to build up self-confidence by actively seeking the support of family and friends, even when those relationships can sometimes be rocky. "Even though we get in a lot of fights, my mom is always there to back me up," says Christina, 14.

Notes Elizabeth, 16, "Strong friendships can help you through almost anything, whether it be a girl from school, a sister or brother, or even a parent."

And getting support is critical for girls with any serious problems. "You've got to find someone to talk to that you can trust," says Stephanie, 15. "That's the only way you're going to get help."

So you see? Being Self-ish can be the best thing a girl ever did. And when you're Self-ish in the classroom, school is bound to be great!

Resources *for Girls*

If you want to learn more about ways you can be happier and more successful in school, many programs, organizations, and publications can help.

However, you should call a crisis hotline—such as 1-800-4-A-CHILD—if you feel you have a serious problem, including being abused, using drugs or alcohol, being depressed, getting pregnant, or running away from home. The yellow pages of your telephone book list local resources under "Crisis Intervention." Phone numbers with an 800 or an 888 area code are toll free.

Organizations—Mentors and Girl Groups

Volunteers at Big Sisters spend time with and mentor girls. Some chapters offer a "Life Choices" program that helps girls make the best decisions for themselves. You can also look in your phone book for a local Big Brothers Big Sisters number.

> Big Brothers Big Sisters of America
> 230 North 13th Street
> Philadelphia, PA 19107
> (215) 567-7000
> www.bbbsa.org

Girls, Incorporated has many local chapters where girls gather for fun and learning, with programs such as Operation SMART for math and science enrichment, and Friendly PEER-suasion, in which girls help others resist drugs and alcohol.

> Girls, Incorporated
> 30 East 33rd Street
> New York, NY 10016
> (212) 689-3700
> www.girlsinc.org

Girl Scouts go way beyond camping these days and offer lots of fun learning experiences, especially in nontraditional areas like math and science. A contemporary issues program helps girls learn about self-esteem, health issues, good relationships, stress management, and other topics. The national office can help you find a local troop.

Girl Scouts of the USA
420 Fifth Avenue
New York, NY 10018-2702
(212) 223-0624
www.gsusa.org

After-school YWCA clubs include GEMS, a math and science booster, and PACT, a peer education program in which girls learn to teach other girls about health and sexuality issues, about how to resist peer pressure, and about how to be a leader.

YWCA of the USA
726 Broadway
New York, NY 10003
(800) YWCA-US1
www.ywca.org

Organizations—Self-Esteem and Body Image

The National Association to Advance Fat Acceptance (NAAFA) can help you accept and like the body you have, whether you're overweight or normal-sized but think you're fat. NAAFA offers information and can refer you to local groups.

NAAFA
Post Office Box 188620
Sacramento, CA 95818
(800) 442-1214
www.naafa.org

The National Eating Disorders Organization (NEDO) offers free information about anorexia, bulimia, and exercise addiction and makes local referrals for treatment.

NEDO
6655 South Yale Avenue
Tulsa, OK 74136
(918) 481-4404
www.laureate.com

Organizations—Sexuality and Body Changes

You can contact the National Gay and Lesbian Task Force (NGLTF) for a referral to a local support group or organization for lesbian, gay, bisexual, and transgender young people.

NGLTF
1700 Kalorama Rd NW
Washington, DC 20009
(202) 332-6483
www.ngltf.org

Planned Parenthood helps with questions about birth control, pregnancy tests, abortion, and sexuality counseling. They can send information. Dialing (800) 230-PLAN automatically connects you with the nearest clinic. Some areas offer a peer education service for girls.

Planned Parenthood Federation of America
810 Seventh Avenue
New York, NY 10019
(800) 829-7732
www.plannedparenthood.org

The Sex Information Education Councils will refer you to local organizations that can help with questions about the body, sex, and pregnancy.

> Sex Information Education Councils of the United States
> 130 West 42nd Street, Suite 350
> New York, NY 10036
> (212) 819-9770
> www.siecus.org

Magazines and Newspapers

Blue Jean, a magazine for older girls, focuses on publishing what young women are "thinking, saying, and doing."

> *Blue Jean*
> Post Office Box 507
> Victor, NY 14564
> (716) 924-4080
> www.bluejeanmag.com

New Girl Times is a national newspaper for girls. It has "all the news that's fit to empower."

> *New Girl Times*
> 215 West 84th Street
> New York, NY 10024
> (800) 560-7525

New Moon is a bimonthly magazine that has news and fiction for and about girls. *New Moon* is planned by an editorial board of girls aged nine to fourteen and has lots of things written and drawn by girls.

> *New Moon: The Magazine for Girls and Their Dreams*
> Post Office Box 3587
> Duluth, MN 55803
> (800) 381-4743
> www.newmoon.org

Teen Voices is a quarterly magazine written by teen girls about lots of good topics including body image, media stereotyping of girls, racism, sexual abuse, and family relationships. Each issue usually has fiction and poetry, too.

    Teen Voices
    Post Office Box 120027
    Boston, MA 02112-0027
    (800) 882-TEEN
    www.teen voices.com

YO!, a quarterly newspaper, is not just for girls, but it has plenty of writing by girls on a wide range of topics important to teens.

    YO!
    450 Mission Street, Suite 204
    San Francisco, CA 94105
    (415) 243-4364

Websites

FeMiNa—at www.femina.com—has a section for girls that includes information on books, careers, games, health, sports, music, technology programs, and links to girls' homepages.

Girl Power—at www.health.org/gpower—has all kinds of subcategories, including a new one on body image, to go along with information on eating right, staying active, and respecting your body.

GirlTech—at www.girltech.com—encourages girls to explore the world of technology. Subcategories include a bulletin board, tech trips, girl views, cool games, and girls in sports.

Girl Zone—at www.girlzone.com—is governed by a teen advisory board and shares information on books, health, and self-image.

Troom—at www.troom.com—offers information on travel, music, issues, and body changes.

Books

Abner, Allison, and Linda Villavosa. *Finding Our Way: The Teen Girls' Survival Guide.* New York: HarperPerennial, 1996.

Driscoll, Anne. *Girl to Girl: The Real Deal on Being a Girl Today.* Rockport, MA: Element, 1999.

Gadeberg, Jeanette. *Brave New Girls: Creative Ideas to Help Girls Be Confident, Healthy, and Happy.* Minneapolis, MN: Fairview Press, 1997.

Girls Know Best: Advice for Girls from Girls on Just About Everything. Hillsboro, OR: Beyond Words, 1997.

Harlan, Judith. *Girl Talk: Staying Strong, Feeling Good, Sticking Together.* New York: Walker, 1997.

Jukes, Mavis. *It's a Girl Thing: How to Stay Healthy, Safe, and in Charge.* New York: Knopf, 1996.

Sandler. Sara. *Ophelia Speaks: Adolescent Girls Write about Their Search for Self.* New York: HarperCollins, 1999.

Resources
for Parents and Teachers

Organizations
The American Association for the Advancement of Science (AAAS) sponsors many programs for teachers, such as Girls and Science.

    AAAS
    1200 New York Avenue NW
    Washington, DC 20005
    (202) 326-6400
    www.aaas.org

The catalog of the American Association of University Women (AAUW) lists publications and videos that suggest how to make classrooms fair for girls, that encourage girls in nontraditional areas, and that give advice on handling issues such as sexual harassment. AAUW also sponsors Sister-to-Sister girls' conferences around the country.

    AAUW
    1111 16th Street NW
    Washington, DC 20036
    (202) 785-7700
    (call (800) 326-AAUW for catalog)
    www.aauw.org

The Math/Science Network looks for ways to draw more women into scientific careers. One of its programs is called EQUALS. It offers workshops, programs, and publications that teachers can use to increase the numbers of girls who take math and science classes.

> EQUALS
> Lawrence Hall of Science
> University of California at Berkeley
> Berkeley, CA 97420
> (510) 642-1823
> www.lhs.berkeley.edu/equals/EQhomeFrm.htm

Girls, Incorporated provides a variety of resources to teachers, including Operation SMART, a program that encourages girls in science, math, and technology.

> Girls, Incorporated
> 30 East 33rd Street
> New York, NY 10016
> (212) 689-3700
> www.girlsinc.org

The National Coalition of Girls' Schools (NCGS) offers information about girls-only schools in the United States, Canada, and Australia. It sponsors teacher workshops and girl-friendly programs such as math and science enrichment.

> NCGS
> 228 Main Street
> Concord, MA 01742
> (508) 287-4485
> www.ncgs.org

The National Foundation for the Improvement of Education provides services to individuals and groups who are addressing sex discrimination in schools.

> National Foundation for the Improvement of Education
> 1201 16th Street NW
> Washington, D.C. 20036
> (202) 822-7840
> www.nfie.org

The National Women's History Project has plenty of information and resources about our foremothers. The organization offers a catalog and has a website.

> National Women's History Project
> 7738 Bell Road
> Windsor, CA 95492
> (707) 838-6000
> www.nwhp.org

The Women's College Coalition has a website—called Expect the Best from a Girl—to visit for resources and tips on helping girls get the most out of school.

> Women's College Coalition
> 125 Michigan Avenue NE
> Washington, DC 20017
> (202) 234-0443
> www.academic.org

The Women's Educational Equity Act (WEEA) will send a free catalog with plenty of resources for classroom fairness, self-esteem growth, and girl-friendly classroom materials.

> WEEA
> Equity Resource Center
> EDC 55 Chapel Street
> Newton, MA 02458
> (800) 225-3088
> www.edc.org/womensequity

Books

Bingham, Mindy. *Things Will Be Different for My Daughter: A Practical Guide to Building Her Self-Esteem and Self-Reliance.* New York: Penguin, 1995.

Eagle, Carol. *All That She Can Be: Helping Your Daughter Achieve Her Full Potential and Maintain Her Self-Esteem during the Critical Years of Adolescence.* New York: Simon & Schuster, 1993.

How Schools Shortchange Girls: An AAUW Report. Washington, D.C.: National Education Association, 1995.

Mann, Judy. *The Difference: Discovering the Ways We Silence Girls.* New York: Warner, 1996.

Odean, Kathleen. *Great Books for Girls: More than 600 Books to Inspire Today's Girls and Tomorrow's Women.* New York: Ballantine, 1997.

Orenstein, Peggy. *SchoolGirls: Young Women, Self-Esteem, and the Confidence Gap.* New York: Bantam Doubleday, 1995.

Pipher, Mary. *Reviving Ophelia: Saving the Selves of Adolescent Girls.* New York: Ballantine, 1995.

Sadker, Myra and David Sadker. *Failing at Fairness: How Our Schools Cheat Girls.* New York: Touchstone, 1995.

Thorne, Barrie. *Gender Play: Girls and Boys in School.* New Brunswick, NJ: Rutgers University Press, 1993.

Index

About the Author

Helen Cordes has had a longtime interest in girls' and women's issues. The mother of two daughters, she writes for magazines such as *Parenting*, *New Moon*, and *The Nation* and volunteers at a Montessori school. In the past, Cordes has served as a staff editor at the *Utne Reader* and has worked as a College Press Service reporter. She lives in Georgetown, Texas, with her husband, Eric, and their daughters, Jesse and Zoe. *Girl Power in the Mirror* and *Girl Power in the Classroom* are her first books.

50110120560

J   Cordes, Helen.
373.18
COR   Girl power in the
           classroom

HIC *			

Discarded
Maury Co Public Library

Blue Grass Regional Library
Columbia, Tennessee 38401